Learning Points

- Animals fascinate young children and it is a special treat to see baby animals. It's exciting for children to recognise and learn about animal families in their own books.

- This book is designed to help you talk together about baby animals and their parents as well as introducing your child to some simple facts about them.

- Take time to look at the details in the pictures. Can your child remember what the animals and their babies are called?

- What other animals can you think of to talk about?

Ladybird books are widely available, but in case of difficulty may be ordered by post or telephone from:

Ladybird Books – Cash Sales Department
Littlegate Road Paignton Devon TQ3 3BE
Telephone 01803 554761

A catalogue record for this book is available
from the British Library

Published by Ladybird Books Ltd Loughborough Leicestershire UK
Ladybird Books Inc Auburn Maine 04210 USA

let's look at
Baby
Animals

by Karen Bryant-Mole
illustrated by Stuart Trotter

Ladybird

Horses and foals

Here is a mother horse and her baby foal. Foals can stand up soon after they are born.

Can you see the diamond shape
on the foal's head?

Goats and kids

These naughty goats have escaped from the field. Goats think flowers are sweet and delicious!

What do you think the farmer
will say?

Sheep and lambs

These lambs are having fun in the spring sunshine.
Can you see one of the lambs feeding from its mother?

Mother sheep often have two or three babies.

Swans and cygnets

Look at these swans gliding down the river. Baby swans are called cygnets. They have light brown feathers. Grown-up swans are white.

Can you see one of the cygnets
sitting on its mother's back?

Dogs and puppies

This mother dog has a busy
time looking after her
playful puppies.

One of the puppies is chasing
her own tail.
Do you think she will catch it?

Cats and kittens

These hungry kittens are drinking milk. They use their little pink tongues to lap it up. Mother cat is cleaning her paws.

Most of the kittens are the same colour. Which one is different?

Hens and chickens

When a hen lays an egg, she sits on it to keep it warm. A few weeks later a chick hatches. This little chick has just pecked his way out of his shell.

Can you make a noise like a chick?

Cows and calves

The cow and her calf are in the barn. Newborn calves drink only milk.

Cows like eating grass.
Have you ever seen a cow?

Ducks and ducklings

Look at the mother duck and her ducklings swimming across the pond. The little boy is throwing bread to the ducks.

One of the ducks is diving underwater. Can you see her tufty tail?

Pigs and piglets

The mother pig in this sty has some piglets. Look at all the curly pink tails!

How many piglets can you count? What a lot of noise they must make!

Lions and cubs

Lions often live in big families
called prides. The lion cubs
love to play.
Do you like to play, too?

Can you see the father lion?
He has long thick fur on his head
and neck.

Kangaroos and joeys

Baby kangaroos are called joeys. Newborn joeys are very tiny. They are only about the size of your little finger.

Can you see a joey having a ride
in her mother's pouch?